Country Friends, City Friends

by Christine Wolf
illustrated by C.D. Hullinger

Scott Foresman
is an imprint of

PEARSON

Glenview, Illinois • Boston, Massachusetts • Chandler, Arizona
Upper Saddle River, New Jersey

It was an exciting day! The sun was shining, and the buildings in the city looked tall and shiny.

Tasha's teacher was going to tell the class about a new project. Tasha felt like she had been waiting forever!

Mrs. Jennings pointed to a map on the computer monitor. "Everyone is going to get a new friend to e-mail. Your new e-pal will not be from our school. Your new e-pal will be from a small school in a rural town."

"What's rural?" asked Thomas.

"*Rural* means out in the country," said Mrs. Jennings. "We live in the city . . . that's called urban living. Our new friends will be from a rural farming town."

Tasha had never known she was from an urban environment. She just always said, "I'm from the city." Tasha had never known anyone from the country. All her friends and relatives were from the city. Tasha was excited to start writing to her new rural friend. What would her new e-pal be like?

Tasha wondered, "What should I write to my e-pal?"

Mrs. Jennings seemed to read Tasha's mind. She told the class, "Why not try telling your e-pal about yourself?"

"Dear E-Pal,

Hi. My name is Tasha. I am writing to you from my school in the city. I live with my mom and dad. I also have an older brother. He's in high school. I have a cat named Jasper. Do you have any pets? Please e-mail me!

Your e-pal,
Tasha"

Two days later, Tasha had still not heard from her e-pal. She tried to imagine what her new friend was like. Did her e-pal live on a farm? What did her e-pal do for fun?

"Dear E-pal,

I hope you got my last e-mail. I can't wait to hear from you. Do you have chores? My chores are to unload the dishwasher, clean Jasper's litter box, take out the trash, and help with dinner. At school, I like math, reading poetry, and recess! I get lots of homework. Do you?

Your e-pal,
Tasha"

Finally, Tasha received a reply.

"Dear Tasha,

Hi! My name is Henry. I like having an e-pal. Your life sounds fun. I visited your city once. It's big! I live on a farm. We raise pigs. Have you ever been to a farm? My dad and mom are in charge of everything, but I help out a lot. I have four brothers and one sister and we all have chores. I like the same things in school that you do! We get lots of homework too! Write back soon!

Henry"

Tasha told Mrs. Jennings, "He lives on a farm, and I live in the city, but we like some of the same stuff."

Mrs. Jennings said, "Tasha, you might be surprised. Rural and urban children may share many things."

Tasha got right to work asking Henry more questions.

"Dear Henry,

What are your friends like? My best friend lives two floors above me. I take an elevator to her apartment. We play and do homework together. I like her because she's funny and smart. Write back really soon!

Tasha"

"Dear Tasha,

Wow! You take an elevator to see your friend? You're lucky! My best friend lives next door, but that's three miles away! His name is Simon, and he's funny too. His dad raises horses, and we ride them all the time. Write back soon!

Henry"

Mrs. Jennings asked for all eyes on the board.

"Whether you live in an urban environment or a rural one, you use your five senses every day. Let's investigate what our e-pals' favorite things to see, touch, taste, smell, and hear are."

"Dear Henry,
If you used your five senses to pick your favorite things, what would they be? Just fill out this chart and we can compare our favorite things, okay?
Your e-pal,
Tasha"

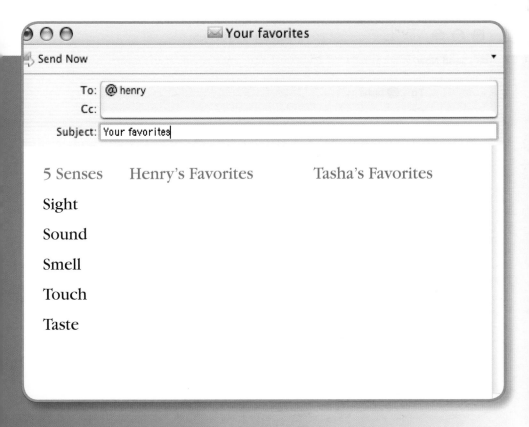

5 Senses	Henry's Favorites	Tasha's Favorites
Sight		
Sound		
Smell		
Touch		
Taste		

"Dear Tasha,
This was fun! I really had to think about my answers. I can't wait to see what your favorite things are.
Your e-pal,
Henry"

Tasha received this e-mail from Henry. She got right to work, filling out her section.

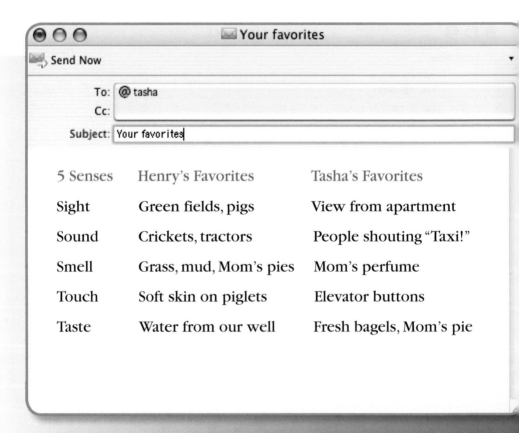

	☒ Your favorites	
Send Now		▾
To:	@ tasha	
Cc:		
Subject:	Your favorites	

5 Senses	Henry's Favorites	Tasha's Favorites
Sight	Green fields, pigs	View from apartment
Sound	Crickets, tractors	People shouting "Taxi!"
Smell	Grass, mud, Mom's pies	Mom's perfume
Touch	Soft skin on piglets	Elevator buttons
Taste	Water from our well	Fresh bagels, Mom's pie

Tasha couldn't believe that Henry liked the smell of mud! She had never thought of mud smelling good before.

She wrote:

"Dear Henry,

Thanks for your e-mail, e-pal! Next time I'm at the park, I'll try smelling some mud. Does it really smell good? It's great that we both like our Mom's pies. I can eat three pieces at a time! I'm glad my teacher asked us to investigate the life of a rural e-pal. I didn't know we'd have so many things in common.

Your urban e-pal,

Tasha"

The next day, Henry was happy to
read Tasha's e-mail. He liked having a
new city friend. He wrote back to her:

"Dear Tasha,

*Hi there! You'll never believe this!
Last night, one of our pigs had a litter
of eleven piglets. They are so sweet. I'm
tired today because I stayed up all night
making sure they were safe and warm.
I'm so happy they are here. I hope
you're having fun…don't do too much
homework!*

Your buddy,
Henry"

The next afternoon, Tasha sent another e-mail to Henry.

"Dear Henry,

That's so cool about the piglets! They must be so cute! I wish I could feel their skin. I hope you get some sleep tonight. My Mom made a pie yesterday, and I thought of you. You're a cool friend, Henry.

Your buddy,
Tasha"

Raising Pigs

Pigs are raised by farmers all over the world.

When a pig is full grown, it can weigh as much as a piano! Grown-up male pigs are called boars. Grown-up female pigs are called sows.

Sows have baby pigs, called piglets. They usually have about eleven piglets at one time.

Piglets like to play-fight when they are very young. They do this to exercise and have fun.

Some pigs live outdoors. They like to wallow in the mud. This keeps them cool and protects their skin.

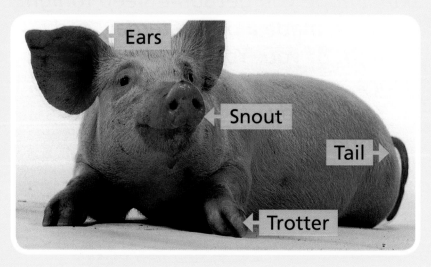

Ears

Snout

Tail

Trotter